Healthy Eating with MyPlate

A Balanced Diet

Catherine Veitch

Heinemann
LIBRARY

Chicago, Illinois

www.capstonepub.com
Visit our website to find out more information about Heinemann-Raintree books.

To order:

☎ Phone 800-747-4992

🖥 Visit www.capstonepub.com to browse our catalog and order online.

Edited by Rebecca Rissman and Adrian Vigliano
Designed by Joanna Hinton-Malivoire
Picture research by Elizabeth Alexander
Originated by Capstone Global Library Ltd.
Production by Victoria Fitzgerald
Printed in the United States of America in North Mankato, Minnesota.
092013   007670RP

15 14 13
10 9 8 7 6 5 4 3

Library of Congress Cataloging-in-Publication Data
Cataloging-in-Publication data is on file at the Library of Congress.

ISBN: 978-1-4329-6994-3 (HC) 978-1-4329-6995-0 (PB)

Acknowledgments
We would like to thank the following for permission to reproduce photographs: © Capstone Publishers p. 4 (Karon Dubke); Getty Images pp. 14 (Jeffrey Coolidge/The Image Bank), 22e (Jeffrey Coolidge/The Image Bank); iStockphoto pp. 7 (© Linda Kloosterhof), 15 (© Nathan Marx); Photolibrary pp. 8 left (Gary k Smith), 12 (VIDAL VIDAL), 19 (Corbis); Shutterstock pp. 6 left (© Mikael Damkier), 6 top right (© Uwe Pilla), 6 bottom right, 22a (© BestPhoto1), 8 right, 22b (© bornholm), 9 (© Monkey Business Images), 10, 22c (© MarFot), 10 inset (© Matka_Wariatka), 11, 13 (© Morgan Lane Photography), 12 inset, 22d (© Lana Langlois), 16 top left (© LockStockBob),16 top right (© raliand), 16 bottom left (© Stephen Orsillo),16 bottom right (© Peter Kirillov), 17 (© Olga Mitsova), 18 top left (© Svetlana Lukienko), 18 top right (© Elnur), 18 bottom left (© taesmileland), 18 bottom right (© val lawless), 20 (© Mandy Godbehear), 21 (© Gabriel Nardelli Araujo); U.S. Department of Agriculture, Center for Nutrition Policy and Promotion p. 5.

Front cover photograph of a girl looking at a large sandwich reproduced with the permission of Corbis (© the food passionates). Back cover MyPlate image courtesy of U.S. Department of Agriculture, Center for Nutrition Policy and Promotion.

Every effort has been made to contact copyright holders of any material reproduced in this book. Any omissions will be rectified in subsequent printings if notice is given to the publisher.

Some words appear in bold, **like this**. You can find out what they mean in "Words to Know" on page 23.

Contents

About this series

Books in this series introduce readers to the importance of a balanced diet and exercise. Use this book to stimulate discussion about where healthy foods come from and how to make healthy food choices.

A Balanced Diet

A **balanced diet** includes fruit, vegetables, grains, **dairy**, and **protein**.

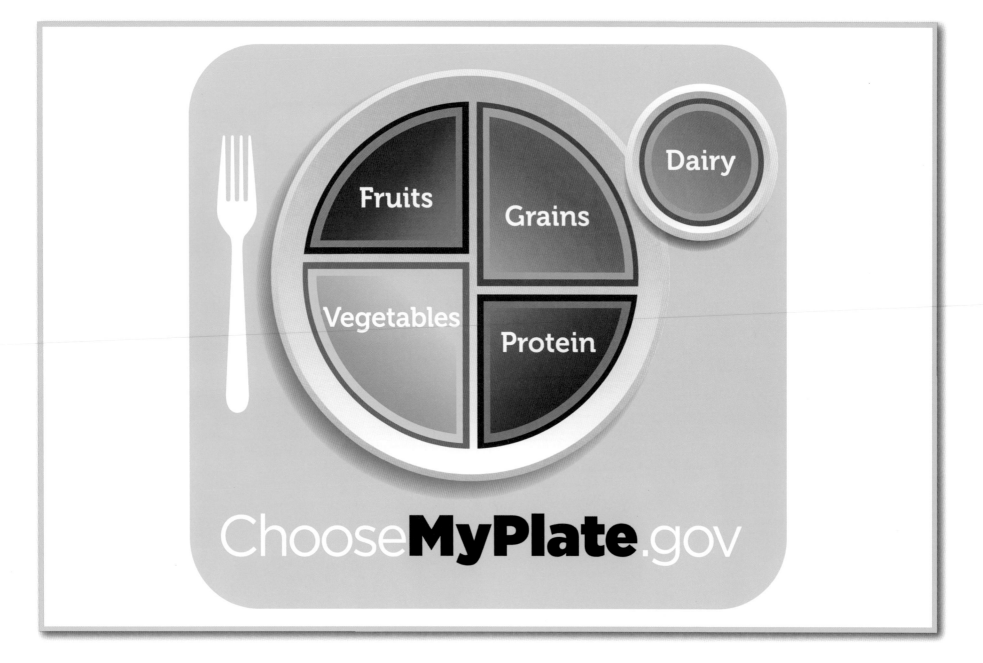

MyPlate shows us the main food groups using a dinner plate and glass. You need to eat or drink foods from each food group to stay healthy. MyPlate shows you how much of each food group to eat.

Fruits

vine

Fruits grow on plants. Apples, tomatoes, and raspberries are fruits. Apples grow on trees. Some tomatoes grow on vines. Raspberries grow on bushes. Eating fruit helps your body fight diseases and keeps you healthy.

Always wash fruit before you eat it.

Most fruits can be picked and eaten as they are. Sometimes fruits are squeezed and made into juice.

Vegetables

peas

A vegetable is a type of plant. Carrots and peas are vegetables. Carrots grow under the ground. Peas grow above the ground.

broccoli

Always wash vegetables before you eat them.

Eating vegetables every day helps keep your body healthy. Some vegetables can be picked and eaten as they are. Some vegetables are cooked.

Grains

oat

oats

Grains are the seeds from some plants. Oats, wheat, and rice are grains. Eating grains every day gives you **energy** and keeps you healthy.

pasta

bread

We make some grains into flour. Bread, pasta, and bagels are made from flour. Some foods are made from whole grains. Make sure that at least half of the grains you eat are made from whole grains.

Dairy

milk

Dairy foods come from milk. We get milk from cows, sheep, and goats. Farmers bring the milk to a dairy. Machines at the dairy prepare the milk. Then milk is put into bottles or cartons.

cheese

yogurt

Milk can be made into different foods. Cheese and yogurt come from milk. Eating different dairy foods every day helps you build strong bones and teeth.

Protein

Protein comes from meat, fish, eggs, beans, and nuts. Meat is a food that comes from animals, such as cows, pigs, and chickens.

Most meat is cooked before it can be eaten. It is important to cook meat well. Eating protein every day helps you to grow.

Healthy Fats

Some fats in our food are good for us. Some fats are bad for us if we eat too much of them. Healthy fats are found in fish, seeds, nuts, and plants. Unhealthy fats are found in cake, cookies, and fried food.

oil

Oils are fats. Some oils come from vegetables or seeds. Some people use oil when they cook food. Oils can also be used on salads. Eating a few oils from foods helps you fight diseases and keeps you healthy.

Sugar

There is a lot of sugar in cookies, candy, soft drinks, and pastries. Too much sugar is bad for your body. To keep your body healthy, you should try to eat only small amounts of sugar.

Too much sugar is bad for your teeth. It is important to brush your teeth after eating sugary foods. You need to clean the sugar off of your teeth.

Exercise and Sleep

As well as eating a **balanced diet**, your body needs regular **exercise**. Regular exercise helps build strong bones and muscles, and a healthy heart.

Your body also needs to rest. Sleep helps you stay strong and healthy. Most children need more than 8 hours of sleep each night.

Can You Remember?

Can you guess which food groups these foods belong to? Look back through the book if you need help.

Answers on page 24

Words to Know

balanced diet diet that includes food from all the food groups. A balanced diet helps keep a body healthy and fit.

dairy place where butter and cheese are made from milk

dairy food made from milk. Cheese, yogurt, butter, and cream are dairy foods.

energy power to do something. We need energy when we work or play.

exercise physical activity that helps keep a body healthy and fit

grains seeds of some plants. Wheat and rice are grains.

oil liquid fat used in food

protein substance in food that gives the body energy and helps it grow. Eggs, meat, nuts, and beans have protein in them.

Index

Answers to quiz on page 22:
a) fruit b) vegetables c) grains d) dairy e) protein

Note to Parents and Teachers

Before reading

Show the children the MyPlate graphic on page 5. Guide children in a discussion about what "balanced" means. Then explain that a balanced diet includes food from all the food groups. Tell children they will learn about the main food groups.

After reading

- As a shared task with the class, write down as many foods as the children can think of in each food group. Ask children if they can think of any foods that are not so healthy.
- Bring in a selection of food magazines (such as free supermarket magazines). Have the children find and cut out pictures of foods from different food groups and put them in separate piles. Give each child a paper plate and ask them to select a picture from each pile to put on their plates to make a healthy meal. Make a wall display of the children's healthy meals.